Whistles Across the Land

A love affair with trains

Photographed by Richard Steinheimer
and Shirley Burman

Written by Richard Steinheimer
with additional quotations by Lucius Beebe,
William Cowper and Francis Bacon

Cedco Publishing Company

My dedication and thanks go to my wife, Shirley and my children, Alan, Marilyn and Sally, who had much to put up with over the years. And to the constant encouragement of my mother, Frances Julian.

Thanks also to some of the professional railroaders of great skill who helped us but do not personally appear in this book. They include Phil Bently, Dick Carter, Al Frazier, Steve LaVigne, Mike Graham, Guadalupe Jimenez, Jim Mahon, Pascual Martinez, Gerald Nester, John Pomykata, Arcadio Ruvalcaba, Chip Savoye and Danny Thiel. Also Mike Pechner, who could forecast the weather.

– Richard Steinheimer 1993

This book is for you Sandy, Sharon, Bill, Tommy and Rick. You suffered through it all while your mom was relentless with her camera, following you all around as you were trying to grow up. Now with my camera I chase after trains, instead of pursuing my children. And love to my soul mate and husband, Dick, who brought me a trainload of rainbows.

– Shirley Burman 1993

First Edition, December 1993

This book is published by Cedco Publishing Company
2955 Kerner Blvd., San Rafael, CA 94901 USA

Printed in Korea

ISBN 1-55912-505-5

STEEL RAILS APPEAR WELDED TOGETHER AT THE HORIZON BY AN APPROACHING TRAIN.
SANTA FE, SELIGMAN, ARIZONA 1983

WHILE STEAM ENGINES WAITED AT ROUNDHOUSES TO BE SERVICED, COLORFUL NEW DIESEL-ELECTRICS
WERE OUT TAKING OVER THE NATION'S RAIL NETWORK.

Contents

Introduction

*T*he inspiration for this book comes from the beautiful and interesting features of American railroading we discovered on our own photographic adventures.

Countless hours were spent waiting for trains or people to appear in optimum lighting conditions, only to have the sun go down, or the clouds depart, well ahead of their arrival. Or we'd climb out of the van in the pre-dawn to capture the first touch of sunlight on the side of a locomotive, only to be disappointed when the train arrived too soon or too late. The raucous call of a raven at such times was enough to give us the strong impression we were being laughed at.

As two railroad photographers in one family, we'd talk in those interludes about assembling some of our more "artful" documentary images into a different kind of railroad book, one that could depict the unusual and interesting lives of railroad people and show the variety of trains and railroad experiences found in this country.

We hope you will enjoy this product of those talks, and that you will gain a bit of insight into the dynamic world of railroading that exists on the periphery of our daily lives. The words accompanying the photographs offer our own poetic and interpretive viewpoints to specific images and the captions provide a few specific details.

Our journeys took us mostly through the West, though we discovered equally interesting stories and pictures along the East Coast where American railroading began in 1828. In addition to the usual photographs of passing trains, we have included images of many less commonly examined elements of American railroading—stations, depots, cars, shops, mixed trains and, most importantly, the men and women doing the hard work that keeps America's railroads in business.

Our inclusion of women railroaders is small compensation for the evidence that they have worked in the industry since its first decade.

We appreciate the assistance received from a number of railroad museum staffers and volunteers, the busy people who keep the heritage of steam and early diesel railroading alive for the benefit of future generations.

The photographs were made on strenuous trips to unusual and often distant locations in the four decades from 1953 to 1993. We believe they represent a unique and authentic contribution to the historic interpretation of railroads in America.

We hope you enjoy the book and will show it to others.

Richard Steinheimer   Shirley Burman

OUT OF WINTER'S STORAGE, SEEING ITS BREATH IN THE COLD, A LONELY
SURVIVOR IS AWAKENED, TO CARRY ON THE STEAM TRADITION.

NEVADA NORTHERN RAILROAD, 1987, PHOTO: SHIRLEY BURMAN

Heritage

A revered heritage of American railroading lies with the great steam locomotives and passenger trains of the first half of this century. In today's uncertain era of collapsing corporate structures and institutional changes, we can look back with pleasure at those trains and the better times we often associate with them.

It was a period of latter-day steam locomotive innovation, urged on by the appearance of the early diesel-electric locomotives on the fast trains of the 1930s. Also, new passenger diesels were not available during World War II when freight locomotives were most needed.

Among the memorable high performance steam passenger locomotives were the big and fast Santa Fe Railway 4-8-4 types inhabiting the stations between San Diego and Chicago. Southern Pacific's beautiful "Daylight" passenger locomotives of the same wheel arrangement first appeared on their namesake Los Angeles to San Francisco train in the 1930s. One of those orange, red and silver locomotives survives today and is seen on business and fan excursions on the lines of the Southern Pacific Railroad.

Steam locomotives helped the nation's railroads carry 90% of all wartime freight traffic and 97% of all military passenger travel. On the mountain grades you could find one-million-pound Cab-forward articulated locomotives and old dinky teakettles working together to move wartime freight.

Today, most steam locomotives are kept alive in spirit and practice by railroad museums, where energetic groups of volunteers help supply the workforce for the constant maintenance and repairs demanded by that very labor-intensive form of motive power.

Among the early railroads using diesel locomotives in passenger service were the Union Pacific and the Burlington Lines. Three Union Pacific Streamliners, co-owned with the Chicago & Northwestern and the Southern Pacific, would race westward from Chicago on their fast 39 3/4 hour schedules to Portland, San Francisco and Los Angeles. Near the end of the life of the Railway Mail Service, the Burlington diesels and Railway Post Office car are pictured before one of their nightly dashes from Omaha to Chicago.

HAVING SEEN THAT PERIOD IN MY YOUTH, IT'S VERY HARD TO BELIEVE THAT THE STEAM LOCOMOTIVE
AND ITS GIGANTIC INFRASTRUCTURE ARE ALMOST TOTALLY GONE.

ADMIRATION IS THE HEART'S NATURAL RESPONSE TO GREAT BEAUTY.

THE ARTFULLY DETAILED STEEL CURVES AND SURFACES, MACHINED AND RIVETED INTO GIGANTIC FUNCTIONAL FORMS, DRIVEN BY THE HIDEOUS POWER OF HIGH PRESSURE STEAM, GAVE THESE LOCOMOTIVES THE VIBRANT, FRIGHTENING PRESENCE THAT WOULD CONQUER CONTINENTS AND CAPTURE THE HEARTS OF MANKIND.

SIERRA RAILROAD, OAKDALE, CALIFORNIA 1992

"SECURE IN THE REPOSITORY OF REMEMBRANCE WHERE NO ACCIDENT OF MISCHANCE OR DERAILMENT HAPPENS, THE TRAINS OF A GOLDEN TIME ROLL TIMELESSLY UPON THEIR APPOINTED ERRANDS, BEYOND REACH OF DELAY BY DISPATCHER OR ANNULMENT BY ANY MANAGEMENT. FOREVER, FOR THEM, THE LIGHTS SHOW GREEN DOWN THE TANGENTS OF GLORY." –LUCIUS BEEBE

UNION PACIFIC NO. 103, 1968

BEFORE THE CREATION OF AMTRAK IN 1971, SLEEPING CARS OF THE CONTINENT'S
CROSSING WERE STILL SUPERVISED BY MEN WEARING THE PROUD BADGE OF OFFICE
OF PULLMAN CONDUCTOR. THE BADGE WAS A HERITAGE OF OLD GEORGE PULLMAN
AND THE CARS THAT CIVILIZED RAIL TRAVEL. THEIR SELF-CONTAINED LIVING AND
SLEEPING QUARTERS WERE DESIGNED FOR COMFORT IN ALL ENVIRONMENTS –
SPACE SHUTTLES OF THE NINETEENTH CENTURY. ANOTHER AMERICAN
TRADITION WAS THE FRIENDLY FAMILIARITY BETWEEN PASSENGERS STRETCHING
THEIR LEGS DURING THE STATION STOPS OF LONG DISTANCE TRAINS.

UNION PACIFIC, CHEYENNE, WYOMING 1968

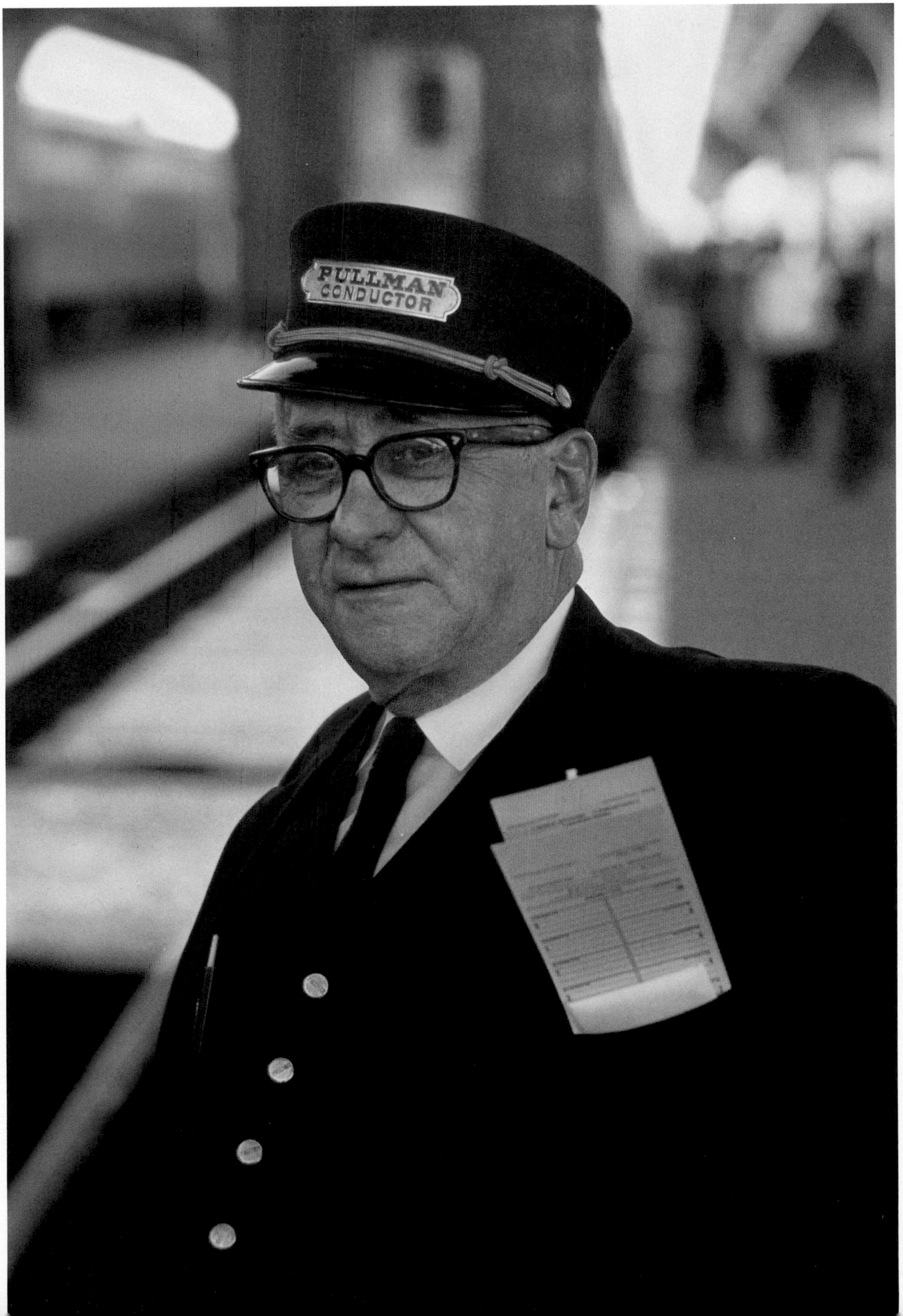

FROM THE EARLY DAYS THROUGH TO THE ELEGANT DOME CAR ERA OF RAILROADING, THE BLACK PULLMAN
PORTER WAS THE UNIMPEACHABLE FRIEND OF SLEEPING CAR PASSENGERS – INTO WHOSE HANDS THE SAFETY
OF GENERATIONS OF YOUNG CHILDREN AND ADULTS WERE REGULARLY ENTRUSTED ON LONG RAIL JOURNEYS.
HE WAS THE INSIGHTFUL GUIDE TO ALL QUESTIONS OF TRAVEL, AS WELL AS MASTER OF THE MYSTERIOUS
MECHANISMS BY WHICH DAYTIME SEATS WERE CONVERTED INTO A NIGHTTIME HOTEL ON WHEELS.

UNION PACIFIC NO. 103, OMAHA, NEBRASKA 1968

UNION PACIFIC NO. 103, OMAHA, NEBRASKA 1968

IN THE LATTER DAYS OF THE RAILWAY MAIL SERVICE AT OMAHA, WE SEE GUN-CARRYING CLERKS SORTING LETTERS AND PACKAGES BEFORE THE 500-MILE DASH OF THEIR RAILWAY POST OFFICE CAR TO CHICAGO. MAIL WILL BE PICKED UP, SORTED AND DELIVERED AT ABOUT A HUNDRED STATIONS ALONG THE WAY.

WITH CARS LIKE THESE ATTACHED TO PASSENGER TRAINS, THE SAME-DAY DELIVERY OF U.S. MAIL BETWEEN PEOPLE 100 OR MORE MILES APART ON A RAILROAD LINE WAS NORMAL MAIL SERVICE FOR THE CENTURY FOLLOWING THE CIVIL WAR. EVEN IN THE HORSE AND BUGGY DAYS, YOUR GREAT-GREAT-GRANDMOTHER COULD TAKE A LETTER TO HER POST OFFICE IN THE MORNING AND KNOW THAT HER SISTER VERA WOULD HAVE IT IN HER POSTAL BOX THE SAME AFTERNOON.

BURLINGTON ROUTE, OMAHA, NEBRASKA 1968

BURLINGTON ROUTE, OMAHA, NEBRASKA 1968

THE GHOSTS OF LITTLE STEAM ENGINES AND TURN-OF-THE-CENTURY PASSENGER CARS
STILL LINGER OVER THE ABANDONED RAILROAD RIGHTS-OF-WAY THAT WIND THROUGH
AEROBICIZED AND COMPUTERIZED AMERICA.

THE *INYO* EQUATION:
WATER + LOGS + FIRE = MOTION.

BEFORE BEING REPLACED BY CENTRALIZED ELECTRONIC DISPATCHING SYSTEMS, TRACKSIDE TRAIN ORDER
OFFICES WERE OUR BEST INFORMATION SOURCES ABOUT RAILROAD OPERATIONS. EVERY DEPOT AND EVERY
TELEGRAPH OPERATOR WAS UNIQUE IN APPEARANCE AND PERSONALITY. YET THEY WERE ALIKE IN THAT THEY
PUT A HUMAN FACE ON THE HIDDEN SECRETS OF RAILROADING AND OPERATING TRAINS. OLDER HEADS
RECALL A DISTANT PAST WHEN THE ONLY POSSIBLE TALK BETWEEN MEN AND WOMEN IN THOSE REMOTE
OUTPOSTS WAS THROUGH THE CHATTER OF DOTS AND DASHES IN A COPPER WIRE.

Across Vast Distances

Today's cross-country trains dash across an America filled with water-soaked meadows and dry, parched deserts, through bright green farmlands and dark evergreen forests. Bridges lift the trains across our largest rivers, and even carry them along the salty shores of the Gulf of Mexico.

But such progress and development always come at a price. If you've ever walked on any of the old pre-railroad wagon trails leading West, you probably felt the hair on the back of your neck rise as you sensed the tremendous life and death decisions that people faced as they left home and committed to the long journey.

The same chill could be felt a century after completion of the first transcontinental railroad by standing along the route where those adventurous men dared to push the rails across the lonely prairies and unknown snowy passes leading to the Pacific Coast.

But by 1968, the wagons that once trailed along near the route of the Union Pacific had become gigantic new diesel locomotives and the old watering holes had become a progression of lonely railroad telegraph offices for delivering orders and messages to the passing trains. The men and women who manned the little depots were part of that old spirit, directing the rush of commerce across a steel trail that disappeared to infinity in both directions.

Today we're denied the pleasant companionship of those people in such distant outposts. Trains today are dispatched from central computerized facilities where a prairie sun must never intrude.

Gone with the winds, also, are the Mixed trains of the midlands. They rode the branchlines to distant farming or forest products towns once important enough for daily freight and passenger train services before the coming of the twin predators: the automobile and the motor truck. Largely for regulatory reasons, railroads continued to haul occasional freight and such local products as dairy milk. They provided for occasional riders in the train's caboose or combination coach. For the passenger, it was a wonderful ride in a time machine - a journey back to the last century when railroading was still a retail business with familiar human faces.

SOUTHERN PACIFIC IN THE SIERRA NEVADA MOUNTAINS, CALIFORNIA

SANTA FE, CAJON PASS, CALIFORNIA, PHOTO: SHIRLEY BURMAN

SOUTHERN PACIFIC, CORDELIA, CALIFORNIA

MCCLOUD, CALIFORNIA

SOUTHERN PACIFIC, DUNPHY, NEVADA, PHOTO: SHIRLEY BURMAN

BURLINGTON NORTHERN, BELTON, MONTANA

BURLINGTON NORTHERN, EAST GLACIER, MONTANA

SOUTHERN PACIFIC, CROCKETT, CALIFORNIA

SOUTHERN PACIFIC, GONZALES, CALIFORNIA

SOUTHERN PACIFIC, MOSEL, NEVADA

OF COURSE THERE ARE JUNKYARDS AND CLOTHESLINES ALONG RAILROAD TRACKS, BUT RAISE YOUR EYES TO SEE THE PEOPLE, THE HOUSES, THE RIVERS, THE TOWNS AND THE VAST EMPTY PLACES THAT MAKE UP AMERICA.

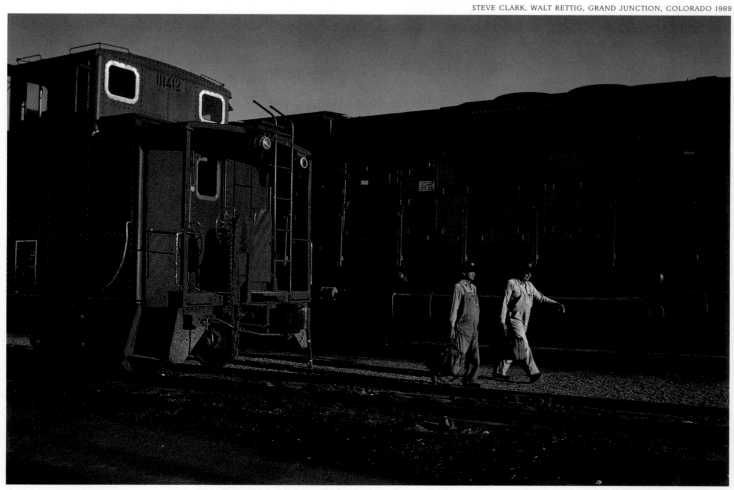

RAILROADING IS STILL A DYNAMIC, CHANGING-TECHNOLOGY INDUSTRY, WHERE LAST YEAR'S BRIGHT IDEAS AND NEW EQUIPMENT ARE ALREADY FADING FROM THE BRILLIANCE OF THIS YEAR'S NEW PERCEPTIONS. THE FEW REMAINING CABOOSES WAIT AT LARGE TERMINALS FOR SPECIAL ASSIGNMENTS. ANOTHER GREAT ICON OF RAILROADING, THE COUNTRY DEPOT, SELDOM SURVIVES UNDER RAILROAD OWNERSHIP PAST THE FADING SOUNDS OF THE LAST DEPARTING TRAINS.

"WOODY" SOUTHERN PACIFIC, LONE PINE, CALIFORNIA 1983

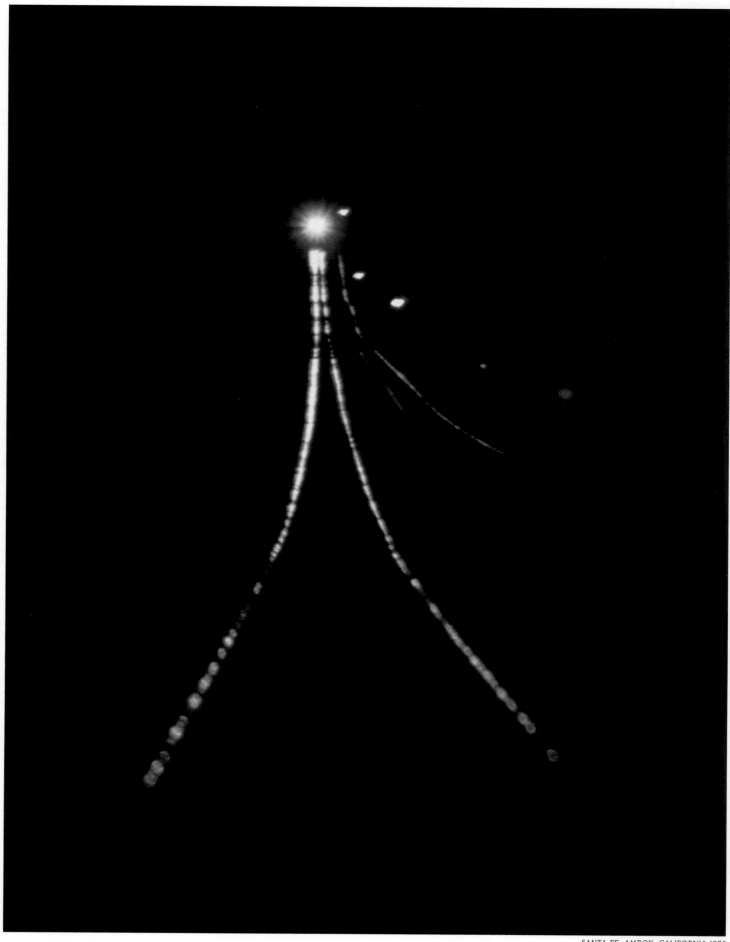

SANTA FE, AMBOY, CALIFORNIA 1976

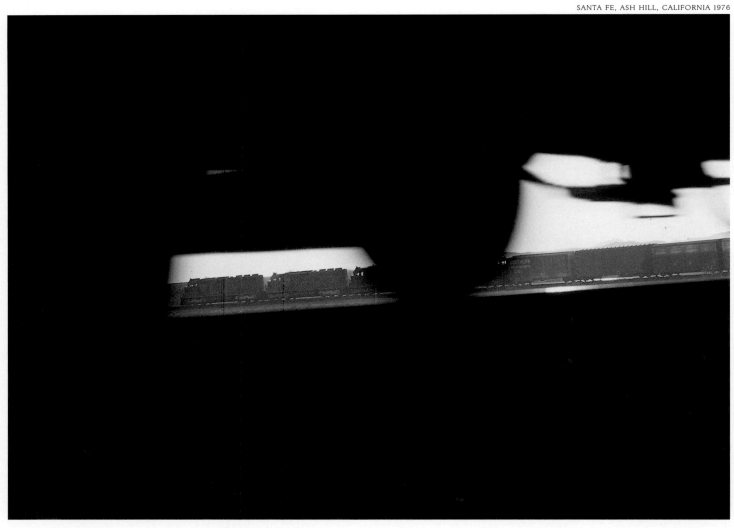

THE GREAT TRAINS RACE ACROSS THE CONTINENT, FLYING LOW ABOVE THE CROSSTIES,
BALANCED ON TWO SHINING STEEL RIBBONS, HELD TAUT BETWEEN THE SEACOASTS.

SOUTHERN PACIFIC, DUNPHY, NEVADA 1985, PHOTO: SHIRLEY BURMAN

CHICAGO AND NORTH WESTERN RAILWAY, HERSHEY, WISCONSIN, 1985

THE LOW, HOT AFTERNOON SUN SKIMS AN ORANGE BEAM ACROSS THE OPEN FLATLANDS OF MIDDLE AMERICA,
ITS MICROSCOPIC RAYS SEARCHING OUT THE TRUE SURFACES OF MEN AND THEIR MACHINES.

THERE IS NO SHORTAGE OF NATURAL LIFE FORMS AROUND RAILROADS. BEHIND THE ENGINE HOUSE YOU'LL FIND THE PERENNIAL CROP OF SEEDLINGS AND BABY BUGS ARISING FROM THE PILES OF DISCARDED LOCOMOTIVE COMPONENTS LYING OUTDOORS ON THE ELEMENTAL EARTH. FROM A GREATER DISTANCE, WE OBSERVE THE SLOW SNAKE-LIKE MOVEMENTS OF A LONG TRAIN FOLLOWING THE OLD SANTA FE TRAIL.

SIERRA RAILROAD, CALIFORNIA 1984, PHOTO: SHIRLEY BURMAN

NEVADA STATE RAILROAD MUSEUM, 1980, PHOTO: SHIRLEY BURMAN

SANTA FE, CROZIER CANYON, ARIZONA 1983

THE PHYSICAL HEROES OF RAILROADING ARE THE MEN WHO MAINTAIN THE TRACK, STRUGGLING
TO HANDLE THE HEAVY CROSSTIES AND STEEL RAILS UPON WHICH THE TRAINS ROLL. FILLING
OUT THE REST OF THEIR TIME, THEY FIGHT SNOW, FIRES, WINDSTORMS, WRECKS, FLOODS AND
AVALANCHES. IF RAMBO WERE A RAILROADER HE'D BE A TRACK MAINTENANCE BOSS.

SOUTHERN PACIFIC, GREAT SALT LAKE, UTAH 1986

SOUTHERN PACIFIC, PALO ALTO, CALIFORNIA 1983

UNION PACIFIC, VICTOR, IDAHO 1968

LOST TO OUR EARS TODAY IS THE TERM, "MIXED TRAIN," ONE CARRYING BOTH FREIGHT AND PASSENGERS. AS LATE AS THE 1960S, A FEW SERVICE-MINDED RAILROADS STILL SCHEDULED THEM ON COUNTRY BRANCHLINES. PASSENGERS RIDING THE WORN SEATS OF AN OLD CABOOSE OR PASSENGER CAR FOUND THEMSELVES IN A PRE-AUTOMOBILE WORLD, THEIR LITTLE TRAIN CREEPING THROUGH TINY HAMLETS AND UNSPOILED GRASSY FARMLANDS, STOPPING AT EACH DEPOT AND MILK LOADING PLATFORM. ENTERTAINMENT WAS ALMOST INEVITABLY PROVIDED AT THE END OF THE LINE. THE TRAIN HAD TO BE TURNED AND PASSENGERS FOUND THEMSELVES INVOLUNTARY PARTICIPANTS IN THE WALK TO A VILLAGE RESTAURANT OR SIGNIFICANT COUNTRY EVENTS SUCH AS CATTLE ROUNDUPS AND LIVESTOCK AUCTIONS.

WARREN MARCUS, UNION PACIFIC, VICTOR, IDAHO 1968

ON A FOGGY MORNING IN THE NORTHERN PLAINS, A LONE ENGINEMAN LEAVES A COUNTRY DEPOT
TO WALK OUT THROUGH THE MISTS TOWARD HIS LOCOMOTIVES – PREPARED FOR TODAY'S JOB
OF MAKING STARTS AND STOPS FOR A MAINTENANCE GANG DUMPING ROCK BALLAST.

CHICAGO AND NORTH WESTERN RAILWAY HUDSON, MINNESOTA 1985

YOU DRIVE A COUPLE OF MILES EAST OF TOWN TO SEE A FAVORITE SIGHT, RARE ANYWHERE BUT IN THE SOUTHWEST DESERTS. LOOKING BACK DOWN THE HILL, YOU SEE THE TWELVE SHIMMERING MILES OF GREEN BLOCK SIGNALS LIGHTING THE WAY TO THE BAGDAD SIDING.

MOTHER NATURE HAS HER FURNACE TURNED ON FULL IN CALIFORNIA'S MOJAVE DESERT AT AMBOY WHERE THE THERMOMETER AT ROY'S CAFE IS HEADED FOR 120 DEGREES. ON THE NEARBY SANTA FE MAINLINE, A LITTLE SIDEWINDER HAS GOTTEN HIMSELF STUCK IN MELTED CREOSOTE.

BURLINGTON NORTHERN, BATES, WASHINGTON 1982

THE ROLLING BLACK SILHOUETTE OF THE TRAIN SWEPT ACROSS THE MOON
WITH A MILLION LOUD SQUEAKS, SCREECHES AND CLANGS. MOMENTARY IMAGES
OF THE FULL MOON FLASHED STROBOSCOPICALLY THROUGH THE GAPS BETWEEN
THE LOUD, FAST MOVING CARS.

WITH A FINAL "WHAM!," THE LAST CAR OF THE TRAIN ROARED PAST, RETURNING
THE MOON AND THE RIVER BACK AGAIN TO CONSTANT VIEW. THE SIGHTS AND
THE NOISE HAD BEEN DISORIENTING; THERE WAS BARELY TIME TO CAPTURE
THE IMAGE OF THE YELLOW BLOCK SIGNAL BEHIND THE QUICKLY RECEDING
TRAIN.

BURLINGTON NORTHERN, SPOKANE, WASHINGTON 1982

SOUTHERN PACIFIC SHOPS, SACRAMENTO, CALIFORNIA 1989

ALL OF THE HUGE STEAM LOCOMOTIVE SHOPS OF NORTH
AMERICA ARE GONE, OR ENGAGED IN THE REPAIR OF CON-
TEMPORARY DIESEL LOCOMOTIVES. BUT FOR MORE THAN A
CENTURY, THOSE SHOPS IN PLACES LIKE PHILADELPHIA,
OMAHA, ALTOONA, ROANOKE AND SACRAMENTO WERE GREAT
"COLLEGES OF CRAFTSMEN." SKILLED WORKERS AND
APPRENTICES OF NEARLY EVERY PROFESSION COULD
PAINSTAKINGLY CONVERT EVEN RAW TREE TRUNKS AND
STEEL INGOTS INTO BEAUTIFULLY DESIGNED AND FINISHED
STEAM LOCOMOTIVES AND CARS. THEY BUILT ABSOLUTELY
ANYTHING THEY NEEDED ALONG THE WAY – EVEN DOWN TO
DOORLOCK FACE PLATES. NOW THOSE OLD WORKERS AND
NEARLY EVERYTHING THEY CONSTRUCTED ARE GONE, VIC-
TIMS OF STANDARDIZED MASS PRODUCED PRODUCTS.
THOUSANDTHS-OF-A-SECOND DIGITAL PULSES HAVE DIS-
PLACED THE SLOW BEAT OF THE DROP-HAMMER AND THE
CRAFTSMEN WITH IT.

UNION PACIFIC, OMAHA, NEBRASKA 1968

UNION PACIFIC, BUFORD, WYOMING 1968

UNION PACIFIC, KINGS CANYON, COLORADO 1968

OH, FOR THE SIMPLE LIFE – TO HAVE OUR OWN LITTLE BOXCAR HOME ON THE RANGE. TO SHARE IT
WITH A CAT OR TWO, AND TO BE ABLE TO LIE IN BED AT NIGHT AND HEAR THE ANCIENT WOODEN
BOARDS AND METAL PANELS TELL ABOUT ALL THE RAILS THEY TRAVERSED IN THEIR YOUTH.

SINCE MOST RAILROADS NEVER THREW AWAY ANYTHING OF CONCEIVABLE MECHANICAL VALUE, ONE LEARNS
A LOT ABOUT THEIR HISTORY BY JUST WALKING AROUND BEHIND THEIR SHOPS.

SANTA FE, SAN DIEGO, CALIFORNIA 1991, PHOTO: SHIRLEY BURMAN

THE FIRST THING THE AVERAGE PERSON NOTICES ABOUT AN OLD DEPOT IS THE NATURE OF ITS ANTIQUITY. THE FURNITURE IS SOLID AND OLD, THE SEATS POLISHED BY THE REAR ENDS OF A MILLION VACATIONERS, SALESMEN AND BUSINESS PEOPLE. EVERYTHING IS THE HANDIWORK OF ARTISANS WHO BUILT FOR THE MILLENNIA – FURNISHINGS AND DECORATIONS A PHARAOH WOULD RECOGNIZE – HANDED DOWN FROM THE DISTANT AGE WHEN THE WORDS "TRAIN" AND "TRAVEL" HAD THE SAME MEANING.

UNION STATION, OMAHA, NEBRASKA 1968

SOUTHERN PACIFIC, SACRAMENTO, CALIFORNIA 1990

UNION STATION, WASHINGTON, DC 1993, PHOTO: SHIRLEY BURMAN

BURLINGTON NORTHERN, LIVINGSTON, MONTANA 1988

UNION STATION, CHICAGO, ILLINOIS 1985

UNION PACIFIC, EVANSTON, WYOMING 1968

UNION PACIFIC, SIDNEY, NEBRASKA 1968

UNION PACIFIC, LOOKOUT, WYOMING 1968

A CENTURY OF PASSAGE BY COAL-BURNING
UNION PACIFIC STEAM LOCOMOTIVES HAS LEFT
A RAIN OF BLACK CINDERS ACROSS THE MID-
LANDS OF AMERICA THAT STILL LINGERS AT
TRACKSIDE BENEATH THE GRASSES AND SAGE-
BRUSH. LONG GONE ARE THE FREIGHT WAGONS
AND THE BUFFALO HERDS THAT ONCE BLOCKED
THE RAILS. IT'S 1968 AND COMMERCE RACES
ACROSS THIS FIRST TRANSCONTINENTAL LINE
BEHIND HUGE, TIRELESS LOCOMOTIVES WITH THE
POWER OF 5,000 SIOUX WAR PONIES.

UNION PACIFIC, DALE CREEK, WYOMING 1987, PHOTO: SHIRLEY BURMAN

HOW EXCITING IS THE DASH OF A FAST TRAIN,
PUSHED EASTWARD BY THE LAST RAYS OF SUNLIGHT,
RACING EVEN THE MESSAGES IN THE WIRES.

SANTA FE, LUPTON, ARIZONA 1983, PHOTOS: SHIRLEY BURMAN

RAILROADING IS STILL A FAMILY AFFAIR. TODAY'S WOMAN RAILROADER IS THE ENGINEER OF A
FAST 'HOTSHOT' FREIGHT TRAIN AT CARLIN. WITH A FIRM HAND ON THE THROTTLE, SHE ROARS
EASTWARD ACROSS THE NEVADA DESERT TOWARD HOME IN THE SALT LAKE VALLEY, LEAVING
HER ENGINEER HUSBAND TO GET HOME LATER WITH HIS LONGER AND HEAVIER TRAIN.

SOUTHERN PACIFIC, CARLIN, NEVADA 1987

AMTRAK, BOCA, CALIFORNIA 1989

AMTRAK, COLFAX, CALIFORNIA 1984

A MIRACLE OF OUR AGE IS THAT AMTRAK HAS BEEN
ABLE TO SURVIVE A DECADE OF ATTACKS FROM
WASHINGTON AND STILL EXPAND AND IMPROVE ITS
SERVICE TO THE PEOPLE OF THE COUNTRY WHO NEED
PUBLIC TRANSPORTATION.

THERE IS A CERTAIN BEAUTY IN AMERICA'S NEWEST TRANSCONTINENTAL TRAINS – THE LANDBRIDGE TRAINS THAT CARRY DOUBLE-STACK SHIP CONTAINERS ACROSS THE COUNTRY. THIS TRAIN CROSSING THE COLORADO RIVER INTO THE ARIZONA DESERT MAY BE 3,000 MILES AWAY IN A FEW DAYS, ITS WHEELS THEN GENTLY TRACING THE BEAUTIFUL TWISTING SHORELINE OF NEW YORK'S HUDSON RIVER.

CONRAIL, BEAR MOUNTAIN, NEW YORK 1991

TO SEE THE ACTUAL VIGOR AND PRODUCTIVITY OF RAILROADING, GET OUT
INTO THE COUNTRY WHERE THE REAL WORK'S BEING DONE.

Mountain Grades

The mountain ranges of America provide many fine locations for watching trains. The rugged ascents of the Rocky Mountains and the Sierra Nevada are especially scenic places for observing trains on steep grades. As in the long ascent of the Arizona Divide, trains are stretched out around several curves while the locomotives work dramatically at full throttle.

Mountains are more significant to railroaders than to you in your car because the typical freight train operates with only about 2 horsepower per ton of train, making your one-ton car, with a 100 horsepower engine, fifty times overpowered compared to that fuel-efficient old freight train. Now, even more efficient high horsepower locomotives can climb hills more surely than earlier models.

Though the operation of long trains across the mountains is usually routine, everything changes in the stormy days of winter. The burden of hard work shifts to the maintenance of way crews who must keep the lines open despite every challenge.

On mountain passes with heavy snows, the track crews often work all hours of day and night, personally feeling the pain of 55 mile-per-hour blowing snow, and keeping track switches clear so train operations may proceed normally. In very heavy snow zones, train crews also get very involved in the pushing and shoveling required to keep drifts from accumulating on the rails, running flanger plows to keep snow from getting packed in between the rails where it might cause a derailment.

Probably the most professional of today's railroad snow-fighting crews are those who keep trains moving across Donner Pass in the Sierra Nevada. Despite winters averaging more than 35 feet of snowfall, qualified volunteer trainmen and seasoned maintenance crews keep train operations virtually normal using both flangers and wide-wing Jordan spreaders to push snow away from the tracks. On the adjacent busy I-80 route into California, a heavy storm will often close the highway. While interstate truckers wait for tax-paid state employees to clear the way, the railroad pays for its own snow removal as well as taxes on its own right-of-way.

"THE FROST HURTS NOT WEEDS."–BOOK OF PROVERBS

SANTA FE, SUPAI, ARIZONA 1983, PHOTO: SHIRLEY BURMAN

SOUTHERN PACIFIC, TRUCKEE, CALIFORNIA 1983

MILWAUKEE ROAD, AVERY, IDAHO 1968

DEER LODGE, MONTANA 1968

ADAM GRATZ, ALBERTON, MONTANA 1974

64

COLUMBIA RIVER, WASHINGTON 1974

WHICH RAILROAD IS THIS? AFTER THE MERGER OF FOUR MAJOR RAILROADS INTO THE BURLINGTON NORTHERN RAILROAD IN 1970, TRAINS RACING EASTWARD UP THE GORGE OF THE COLUMBIA RIVER FROM PORTLAND, OREGON, WERE FREQUENTLY PULLED BY WILD COMBINATIONS OF LOCOMOTIVES – EACH ONE PROUDLY PROCLAIMING THE NAME OF ITS PRESENT OR PAST OWNER.

OLD AND FUNKY RAILROADS ARE THE MOST INTERESTING. IN 1915 THE BIG OLD ELECTRIC LOCOMOTIVES OF THE CHICAGO, ST. PAUL AND PACIFIC RAILROAD USED CLEAN HYDRO-ELECTRIC POWER FOR THEIR MONTANA CROSSING. IT WAS THE MOST ADVANCED RAILROAD OF ITS TIME, THE PROTOTYPE FOR SIMILAR MAINLINE ELECTRIFICATIONS IN EUROPE, ASIA, AND IN NORTH AND SOUTH AMERICA. THE OLD ENGINES EVEN RETURNED ELECTRICITY TO THE POWER GRID WHILE DESCENDING MOUNTAIN GRADES. THEY WERE RETIRED DURING THE 1974 ARAB OIL CRISIS, STRANGERS TO A LAND BECOME DEPENDENT ON FOREIGN OIL.

THE MIGHTY SNOWSTORMS THAT TRAPPED AND TORTURED THE 1846 EMIGRANT PARTY LED BY GEORGE DONNER STILL SHOW THEIR MIGHTY FORCE ON THAT SIERRA NEVADA PASS, GIVING TODAY'S AMTRAK PASSENGERS A FEW EXCITING STORIES TO IMPRESS FRIENDS BACK HOME.

JIM GODDARD, SOUTHERN PACIFIC, DONNER, CALIFORNIA 1993

SOUTHERN PACIFIC, CISCO, CALIFORNIA 1983

GARY FERGUSON, SOUTHERN PACIFIC, DONNER, CALIFORNIA 1983

SOUTHERN PACIFIC TUNNEL 6, 1983, PHOTO: SHIRLEY BURMAN

WHEN YOU HEAD OUT OF TOWN WITH 140 TONS OF JORDAN SPREAD-
ERS AND 350 TONS OF LOCOMOTIVES, YOU FEEL YOU CAN HANDLE
ANYTHING. THE RAILROAD STAYS IN FULL OPERATION BECAUSE OF
GOOD LEADERSHIP AND QUALIFIED VOLUNTEER CREWS WHO ENJOY
THE PROFESSIONAL CHALLENGES. ON SNOWY NIGHTS THEY ARE FRE-
QUENTLY REMINDED HOW WELL THEY ARE DOING WHEN THEY LOOK
OUT AND SEE A COMPLETELY DARK INTERSTATE HIGHWAY.

SOUTHERN PACIFIC OIL TRAIN, CAMERON, CALIFORNIA 1988

HUNDRED-TON LOADS OF FOSSIL JUICE
TILTED DOWNGRADE WITH NO CABOOSE,

SLOSHING IN ROUNDED CONTAINERS,
WE'LL TAKE IT DOWN WITH NO RETAINERS,

NO FOOLING AROUND ON THIS HILL,
LOSE CONTROL AND WE'RE IN FOR A SPILL.

FEW CURVES TO HOLD US BACK,
IF WE GO TOO FAST, WE'LL GET THE SACK.

CAN'T TURN THE DYNAMIC LOOSE
IF WITH THIS GRADE WE WANT A TRUCE

SAFELY DOWN WE'LL WAVE TO MAINTAINERS
AND SIP FROM OUR THERMOS CONTAINERS.

JOHN HUNTOON, SOUTHERN PACIFIC, COLTON, CALIFORNIA 1990

THE ENDLESS PARADE OF TRAINS ACROSS AMERICA'S BUSY TRANSCONTINENTAL MAINLINES MAY BE A JOY TO SHIPPERS AND RAILROADERS, BUT NOT ALWAYS TO LINESIDE BUSINESSES. A FEW BOLDLY ENCOURAGE US TO LOOK ELSEWHERE WHEN WE SEEK A LITTLE PLACE TO BE LULLED TO SLEEP BY THE COMFORTING WHIS-TLES OF PASSING TRAINS.

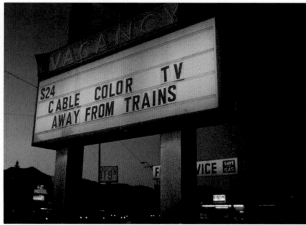

FLAGSTAFF, ARIZONA 1983

ONE THOUSAND EIGHT HUNDRED AND EIGHTY MILES WEST OF CHICAGO, A FLAW HAS DISRUPTED THE SMOOTH FLOW OF TRAINS ACROSS THE SANTA FE'S BUSY TRANSCONTINENTAL MAINLINE. THE WESTBOUND TRACK IS TEMPORARILY CLOSED FOR REBUILDING AT YUCCA, ARIZONA, FORCING TRAINS IN BOTH DIRECTIONS TO USE THE ADJACENT EASTBOUND TRACK.

LIKE A TRAFFIC COP, FLAGMAN BILL DESKIN TAKES CHARGE OF THE CROSSOVER SWITCH, HOLDING WESTWARD TRAINS UNTIL THE DISPATCHER AUTHORIZES HIM TO DETOUR THEM ON THE EASTBOUND TRACK. HE SPENDS THE MORNING HANDING UP WRITTEN TRACK CLEARANCES AND LATER COOKS A NON-GOURMET LUNCH OUTSIDE HIS RED TELEPHONE BOOTH "OFFICE."

A WESTBOUND LOCAL FREIGHT ARRIVES WITH A FRESH TANK OF WATER FOR THE TRACK GANG. WITH HIS SHIRT HANGING OUT AND AN EMPLOYEES' TIMETABLE IN HIS BACK POCKET, THE VETERAN CONDUCTOR OUTLINES A SWITCHING PLAN TO THE WOMAN BRAKEMAN ON THE CABOOSE.

BILL DESKIN, SANTA FE, YUCCA, ARIZONA

C.H. SKINNER, SANTA FE, YUCCA, ARIZONA 1985

BRAKEMAN LAURA PENDLEY, RUNS INTO TROUBLE TRYING TO OPEN THE EXTREMELY STIFF EASTBOUND SIDING SWITCH AT YUCCA FOR HER WORK TRAIN. NOT ASKING FOR ASSISTANCE, NOR GETTING ANY, THIS MODERN WOMAN RAILROADER HANDLES THE SITUATION HERSELF – THROWING THE DIFFICULT SWITCH INTO LOCK POSITION WITH AN IMPRESSIVE DISPLAY OF ATHLETIC STRENGTH.

LAURA PENDLEY, SANTA FE, YUCCA, ARIZONA 1985, PHOTO: SHIRLEY BURMAN

LAURA PENDLEY, SANTA FE, YUCCA, ARIZONA 1985, PHOTOS: SHIRLEY BURMAN

UNION PACIFIC, MINIDOKA, IDAHO 1968

SMALL TOWN DEPOTS GAVE US REGU-
LAR CONTACT WITH THE HUMAN SIDE
OF RAILROADING. BEFORE THE GENER-
AL USE OF AIR TRAVEL, THEY WERE THE
MAIN ENTRY AND DEPARTURE GATE-
WAYS FOR THOSE COMMUNITIES.

DEPOTS WERE THE JUMPING-OFF
PLACES FOR MEN AND WOMEN LEAVING
HOME TO GO TO COLLEGE, TO BIG
CITIES TO FIND WORK, TO MARRY, OR
TO GO TO WAR. THEY WERE PLACES
WHERE FRIENDS CAME TO HELP WAIT
FOR THE TRAIN TO ARRIVE, WHERE
PEOPLE ALWAYS SAID THEIR GOODBYES
WITH A TRACE OF SADNESS – BECAUSE
NOT ALL WHO DEPARTED ALWAYS
RETURNED.

THE COUNTRY WISDOM THAT SEES YOUNG PEOPLE AS IMPORTANT CONTRIBUTORS
TO THE FUTURE IS LESS NOTICED IN THE GREAT CROWDED CITIES OF THE NATION,
WHERE THE GOODBYES OF BOTH PEOPLE AND TRAINS TAKE PLACE BENEATH TALL
AND IMPERSONAL SKYSCRAPERS.

"GREAT PRINCES HAVE GREAT PLAYTHINGS."–WILLIAM COWPER

A love affair with trains

Back on the 1940s and 1950s, in the bedroom community of Glendale, north of Los Angeles, steam-powered trains still had valuable functions to perform and they were the fond objects of many people's attention. On warm nights, one or two dozen people would show up at the SP station for the familiar evening parade of passenger trains.

Two trains could be counted on to have huge Cab-forward locomotives while others would usually have conventional passenger locomotives.

Both kids and adults admired the great steaming locomotives, watched the loading of passengers, and looked at people through the steamy windows of the brightly lit diner. Another object of interest was the conductor, whose brakemen hustled to get people aboard so he could shout his "All Aboard!" command on schedule.

Near the front of the train, people stood in awe of the great steam locomotives and watched the engineer who usually would talk with the crowd or watch the conductor. If a child were terribly lucky or had a dad with connections, they might get hoisted high up into the darkened cab for a brief visit.

Then something would happen each night that was so powerful I can still remember it clearly almost 50 years later. At the moment the conductor gave his signal, everyone near the locomotive would instantly become silent. The only sounds were the panting of the locomotive and the engineer adjusting his valve gear to forward motion, and the rising sound of a steam blower.

Then from deep inside the monster came the first mighty, but very drawn out, chuff of exhaust that slowly got the train inching into motion. That chuff was followed by a second, a third and then an advancing progression of exhausts that became a loud staccato as the rear cars were disappearing into the darkness beyond the depot lights. Usually alone, I remember the ache I would feel in not being aboard that specific train - not being able to lean back in a window seat and listen all night to the rapid exhausts pulling our train north along the coast to those distant and alluring destinations that dwell in a young person's mind.

THE HUNDREDS OF HUGE CAB-FORWARD STEAM LOCOMOTIVES OPERATED BY
THE SOUTHERN PACIFIC RAILROAD WERE UNIQUE TO AMERICA, AND THE MOST
MEMORABLE LOCOMOTIVES OF MANY WESTERN CHILDHOODS. BY THEIR "BACK-
WARD" DESIGN, THEY PROTECTED ENGINE CREWS FROM THE INTENSE EXHAUST
SMOKE IN TUNNELS ON A RAILROAD WITH MORE THAN 30 MILES OF THEM. ONE
LOCOMOTIVE OF THIS TYPE STILL SURVIVES INSIDE THE CALIFORNIA STATE
RAILROAD MUSEUM. TAKING THE PRESERVATION PROCESS EVEN FARTHER WITH
ANOTHER LOCOMOTIVE FROM THE SAME RAILROAD, CAPABLE AND ENTHUSIAS-
TIC VOLUNTEERS IN THE SAN FRANCISCO BAY AREA HAVE RESTORED THE
SMALLER AND MORE CONVENTIONAL NO. 2472 TO FULL OPERATING SERVICE.

NEIL VODDEN, JOHN TESHAHARA, SOUTHERN PACIFIC NO. 2472, 1993

THERE IS A MAGIC ATTRACTION FOUND IN THE TEXTURED MOSAICS OF RAILROAD REFRIGERATOR CARS, AND IN THE WEATHERED WOODEN TIMBERS OF OLD RAILROAD SNOWSHEDS.

SOUTHERN PACIFIC SNOWSHEDS, NORDEN, CALIFORNIA 1985

EVERY MAN HAS A FAVORITE LOCOMOTIVE, BECAUSE, TINY, GIGANTIC OR BEAUTIFUL,
IT EXCEEDS HIS OWN EXPECTATIONS.

STAN GARNER, NEVADA STATE RAILROAD MUSEUM, 1985, PHOTO: SHIRLEY BURMAN

THE BEAUTIFUL STEAM LOCOMOTIVES OF THE NINETEENTH CENTURY MAY LOOK LIKE TOYS TODAY. BUT FOR DECADES THEY WERE THE FASTEST TRANSPORTATION ON EARTH. SO FAST THEY STILL TELL US HOW TO SET OUR CLOCKS.

THEY RACED ACROSS AMERICA WHEN PEOPLE LIVED ON "SUN TIME" – TOWN CLOCKS WERE SET FOR NOON WHEN THE SUN WAS DIRECTLY OVERHEAD, OR OVERHEAD IN A NEARBY CITY. BUT SUN TIME IN THE MIDDLE OF THE NATION CHANGES ABOUT ONE MINUTE FOR EVERY 13 MILES OF EAST/WEST TRAVEL. BECAUSE OF THE SPEED OF THESE ENGINES, WRECKS BEGAN OCCURRING FROM CONFUSION ABOUT THE EXACT TIME OF DAY AT SPECIFIC STATIONS AND MEETING POINTS.

THE ANSWER CAME ON NOVEMBER 18, 1883, WHEN, DESPITE THE PROTESTS OF CITIZENS AND GOVERNMENT OFFICIALS AGAINST 'CHANGING THE LAWS OF NATURE,' THE RAILROADS TOOK AMERICA INTO THE RAILROAD AGE WITH STANDARD TIMEZONES. IT TOOK 35 MORE YEARS FOR THE GOVERNMENT TO MAKE IT LAW.

BLACK MESA AND LAKE POWELL RAILROAD, ARIZONA 1989

P.C. AGGREGATES, DAVENPORT, CALIFORNIA 1961

UNION PACIFIC GAS TURBINE, GRANGER, WYOMING 1968

"THERE IS NO EXCELLENT BEAUTY
THAT HATH NOT SOME STRANGE-
NESS IN THE PROPORTION."
–FRANCIS BACON

NEVADA NORTHERN RAILROAD, ELY, NEVADA 1987

AH, THAT MAGIC TIME JUST BEFORE DAWN – THE MOST QUIET, LOVELY, BEAUTIFUL AND
LEAST OBSERVED PART OF THE DAY.

BURLINGTON NORTHERN, COLUMBIA RIVER, WASHINGTON 1982

SANTA FE, ASH FORK, ARIZONA 1983

SANTA FE, WINSLOW, ARIZONA 1983

CHICAGO AND NORTH WESTERN RAILWAY, ALTOONA, WISCONSIN 1985

TURN AWAY FROM THE INTERSTATE HIGHWAYS AND THE METROPOLITAN AIRPORTS TO FIND THE AMERICA BUILT BY RAILROADS. SEARCH OUT THE OLD ROADS WHERE YOU'LL FIND THE SMALL TOWNS STILL SHOWING THE BIRTHMARKS OF THEIR CREATION.

LIKE BRIDES ON THEIR WEDDING DAY, LOCOMOTIVES NEVER LOOK SO GOOD AS WHEN THEY COME OUT
OF THE SHOPS WITH NEW PAINT.

SOUTHERN PACIFIC, SACRAMENTO, CALIFORNIA 1986

SOUTHERN PACIFIC, SACRAMENTO, CALIFORNIA 1986

THE EMIGRANTS AND THEIR WAGONS HAVE VANISHED INTO TIME. TODAY IT'S THE RAILROADERS WHO TELL
STORIES OF THE SAD MISHAPS AND THE LONELY PLACES OF THE WESTWARD CROSSING.

NEW RAILROAD FANS ARE BEING BORN EVERY DAY.

NO EXPERIENCE BEATS RIDING OUT OF TOWN ON A PRIVATE RAILROAD CAR WITH GOOD FRIENDS!